© 2011   8- 33   11/2014

© 2011   8- 33   11/2014

Biodiversity

of Temperate Forests

GREG PYERS

MACMILLAN
LIBRARY

First published in 2011 by
MACMILLAN EDUCATION AUSTRALIA PTY LTD
15–19 Claremont Street, South Yarra 3141

Visit our website at www.macmillan.com.au or go directly to www.macmillanlibrary.com.au

Associated companies and representatives throughout the world.

National Library of Australia Cataloguing-in-Publication entry

Pyers, Greg.
 Of temperate forests / Greg Pyers.
 ISBN: 9781420278859 (hbk.)
 Biodiversity.
 Includes index.
 For primary school age.
 Forests and forestry—Environmental aspects—Juvenile literature.
 Forest protection—Juvenile literature. Biological diversity—Juvenile literature.

333.75

Publisher: Carmel Heron
Commissioning Editor: Niki Horin
Managing Editor: Vanessa Lanaway
Editor: Georgina Garner
Proofreader: Tim Clarke
Designer: Kerri Wilson
Page layout: Raul Diche
Photo researcher: Wendy Duncan (management: Debbie Gallagher)
Illustrator: Richard Morden (illustration on p. 10 by Alan Laver, Shelly Communications)
Production Controller: Vanessa Johnson

Printed in China

Acknowledgements
The author and publisher are grateful to the following for permission to reproduce copyright material:

Front cover photograph: Two male deer in Park Dyrehaven, Denmark courtesy of photolibrary/Pierre Vernay.
Back cover photographs courtesy of istockphoto/Vladimir Chernyanskiy (wisent); Le Do (leaves).

Photographs courtesy of:
ANTphoto.com.au/Mrs JM Soper, **15**; Corbis/Yann Arthus-Bertrand, **17**, /Raymond Gehman, **27**, **29**; photolibrary/age fotostock/
John Cancalosi, **25**, /Alamy/Jason Edwards, **21**, /Alamy/David Noton, **14**, /Britain on View/Nature Picture Library, **7**, /Gary
Lewis, **4**, /SPL/Bob Gibbons, **9**; Shutterstock/Aleksander Bolbot, **28**, /Sandra Caldwell, **18**, /Steffen Foerster Photography, **22**, /
Jeffrey M Frank, **20**, /Hydromet, **11**, /Henrik Larsson, **23**, /Peter Weber, **13**. Background and design images used throughout
courtesy of Shutterstock/Borislav Gnjidic, (beech forest), /Chukov (autumn trees).

Other material: Maps, US Forestry Service/William B Greeley, **16**.

While every care has been taken to trace and acknowledge copyright, the publisher tenders their apologies for any accidental
infringement where copyright has proved untraceable. They would be pleased to come to a suitable arrangement with the rightful
owner in each case.

Please note
At the time of printing, the Internet addresses appearing in this book were correct. Owing to the dynamic nature of the Internet,
however, we cannot guarantee that all these addresses will remain correct.

Contents

Glossary words

When a word is printed in **bold**, you can look up its meaning in the Glossary on page 31.

What is biodiversity?

Biodiversity, or biological diversity, describes the variety of living things in a particular place, in a particular **ecosystem** or across the whole Earth.

Measuring biodiversity

The biodiversity of a particular area is measured on three levels:

- **species** diversity, which is the number and variety of species in the area
- genetic diversity, which is the variety of **genes** each species has. Genes determine the characteristics of different living things. A variety of genes within a species enables it to **adapt** to changes in its environment.
- ecosystem diversity, which is the variety of **habitats** in the area. A diverse ecosystem has many habitats within it.

Habitats and ecosystems

Temperate forests are habitats, which are places where plants and animals live. Within a forest habitat, there are many smaller habitats, sometimes called microhabitats. Some forest habitats are the forest floor, the tree trunks and the treetops. Different kinds of **organisms** live in these places. The animals, plants, other living things and non-living things and all the ways they affect each other make up a forest ecosystem.

Species diversity

Some habitats, such as coral reefs and rainforests, have very high biodiversity. In one study of a rainforest in Peru, 283 tree species were found growing in just one hectare, or 0.01 square kilometre. In the whole of the United States and Canada, there are just 700 tree species.

Koalas and eucalyptus trees are part of the biodiversity of an Australian temperate forest.

Biodiversity under threat

The variety of species on Earth is under threat. There are somewhere between 5 million and 30 million species on Earth. Most of these species are very small and hard to find, so only about 1.75 million of these species have been described and named. These are called known species.

Scientists estimate that as many as 50 species become **extinct** every day. Extinction is a natural process, but human activities have sped up the rate of extinction by up to 1000 times.

Known species of organisms on Earth

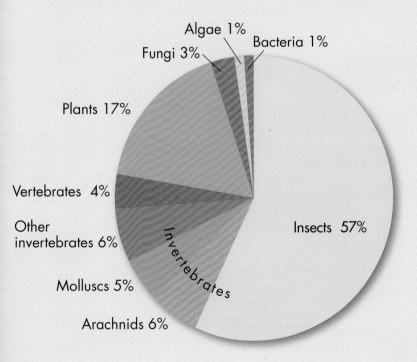

Algae 1%
Bacteria 1%
Fungi 3%
Plants 17%
Vertebrates 4%
Other invertebrates 6%
Invertebrates
Insects 57%
Molluscs 5%
Arachnids 6%

The known species of organisms on Earth can be divided into bacteria, algae, fungi, plant and animal species. Animal species are classified as vertebrates or invertebrates.

Approximate numbers of known vertebrate species

ANIMAL GROUP	KNOWN SPECIES
Fish	31 000
Birds	10 000
Reptiles	8 800
Amphibians	6 500
Mammals	5 500

Why is biodiversity important?

Biodiversity is important for many reasons. The diverse **organisms** in an **ecosystem** take part in natural processes essential to the survival of all living things. Biodiversity produces food and medicine. It is also important to people's quality of life.

Natural processes

Humans are part of many ecosystems. Our survival depends on the natural processes that go on in these ecosystems. Through natural processes, air and water are cleaned, waste is decomposed, **nutrients** are recycled and disease is kept under control. Natural processes depend on the organisms that live in the soil, on the plants that produce oxygen and absorb **carbon dioxide**, and on the organisms that break down dead plants and animals. When **species** of organisms become **extinct**, these natural processes may stop working.

Food

We depend on biodiversity for our food. The world's major food plants are grains, vegetables and fruits, which have been bred from plants in the wild. Wild plants are the source of **genes** for breeding new varieties of plants. These varieties might be bred to be resistant to disease or to be grown in a warmer **climate** or in poor soil. When these plants become extinct, their useful genes are lost.

Medicine

About 40 per cent of all prescription drugs come from chemicals that have been extracted from plants. Scientists discover new, useful plant chemicals every year. The United States National Cancer Institute discovered that 70 per cent of plants found to have anti-cancer properties were rainforest plants. When plant species become extinct, the chemicals within them are lost forever. The lost chemicals may have been important in the making of new medicines.

Did you know?

Walnuts, apples and plums all come from trees that originally grew in temperate forests. Humans have **domesticated** wild fruit and nut trees over thousands of years.

Quality of life

Biodiversity is important to our quality of life. Animals and plants inspire wonder. They are part of our **heritage**. Animals of European temperate forests, such as squirrels, foxes, wolves and badgers, have featured in children's stories for hundreds of years. These stories connect people to the natural world.

Many popular children's stories feature animals of temperate forests, such as foxes. These stories are one example of how biodiversity can inspire our imagination and improve our quality of life.

Extinct species

Ten species of moas once lived in New Zealand forests and other **habitats**. Moas were giant flightless birds. They were preyed on by Haast's eagle, the world's largest eagle. People first arrived in New Zealand around the year 1100, and they hunted the moas to extinction by about 1500. With its prey gone, Haast's eagle also became extinct.

Temperate forests of the world

Temperate forests are found in the temperate zones of the world. In the south, this is the area between the Tropic of Capricorn and the Antarctic Circle. In the north, this is the area between the Tropic of Cancer and the Arctic Circle.

Types of temperate forest

Temperate forests are less dense than rainforests and less open than woodlands. Scientists sometimes define a temperate forest as an area of trees taller than 10 metres, with a **canopy** that covers 50 to 80 per cent of the sky. There are four main types of temperate forest.

Did you know?

Rainforests are a type of dense forest, with a canopy that blocks out more than 80 per cent of the sky. They can be temperate or **tropical**.

Temperate forests are mostly found in the Northern Hemisphere, in North America, Europe and Asia. Some temperate forests are found in southern South America and eastern Australia.

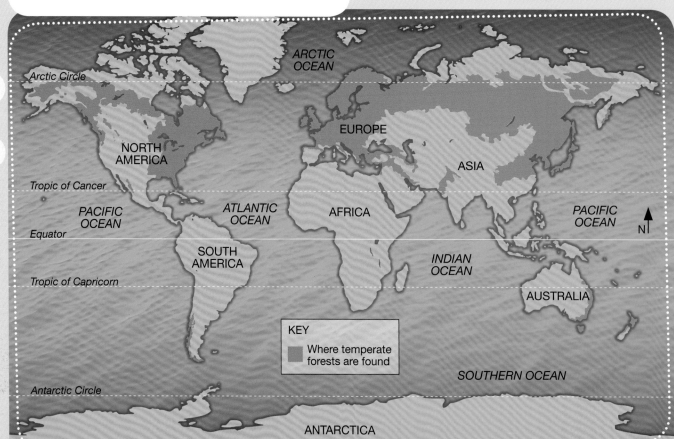

KEY

Where temperate forests are found

Deciduous forest

Deciduous forests have broad-leaved flowering trees, such as oak, elm, plane and poplar. These trees lose their leaves in winter. The deciduous forests of New England, in the eastern United States, are famous for their maple trees, which have leaves that turn a spectacular red in autumn.

Evergreen forest

Evergreen forests have evergreen flowering trees, such as eucalyptus and acacia, which keep their leaves year-round. This type of forest is widespread in southern and eastern Australia. *Eucalyptus regnans*, the world's tallest flowering plant, grows where rainfall is high. Some specimens have grown to more than 90 metres tall.

Coniferous forest

Coniferous forests have conifers, such as redwood, pine and fir, which are cone-bearing trees. These forests are often found in cold **climates**, such as in Norway and Finland. The waxy leaves of conifers help them survive freezing temperatures.

Mixed forest

Mixed forests have a mixture of broadleaf and coniferous trees. The forests of the Adirondacks in New York state, in the United States, have a mixture of deciduous birches and beeches and coniferous red and white pines.

Deciduous leaves and evergreen leaves

Deciduous trees lose their leaves in winter. These leaves are thin and would freeze in the cold weather. Before the leaves fall, useful **nutrients** flow out of the leaves and are stored in the tree's branches and trunk. Evergreen trees in temperate forests have thick, waxy leaves that protect the leaves from freezing. They stay on the tree all year round.

*In this mixed forest in Europe, different **species** of deciduous and evergreen trees may grow side by side.*

Temperate forest biodiversity

Each type of temperate forest has its own biodiversity. **Climate** and soil type influence which tree **species** grow in the forest. In turn, this affects which animal species live there.

Temperate forest layers

A temperate forest has several layers of **vegetation**. The uppermost layer is the **canopy**, which is formed by the leaves and branches of the tallest trees. Beneath this layer is an **understorey** of young trees and shrubs. In moist temperate forests, there may be ferns and mosses. The ground layer, known as the forest floor, is formed by grasses and herbs.

Each layer supports different animal species. In a North American mixed temperate forest, different bird species find their food in different forest layers. Winter wrens search for insects close to the ground, while nuthatches hunt for insects on tree trunks. In the canopy, crossbills feed on pine seeds. Red-tailed hawks soar above the canopy, scanning the ground for prey.

canopy

Temperate forests are made up of three main layers of vegetation.

understorey

forest floor

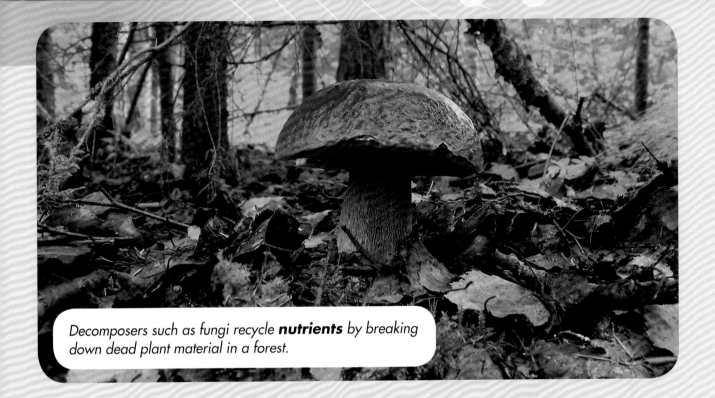

Decomposers such as fungi recycle **nutrients** by breaking down dead plant material in a forest.

Soil types

The type of soil in a temperate forest is important because it affects the biodiversity of the forest. Soil types may be sandy and well drained or rich in clay and poorly drained. They may be **fertile** or infertile, shallow or deep. In southern Australian forests, different types of eucalyptus trees are found in different soils. Messmate trees may be the dominant species on well-drained soils, but where the soil becomes heavier, manna gums may dominate. This affects where koalas can be found, because koalas feed on the leaves of manna gums, but not on messmate leaves.

Decomposing material

Dead material on the forest floor, such as fallen bark and leaf litter, supports a great diversity of **organisms** called decomposers. Decomposers are fungi and invertebrates that feed on dead material and break it down, or decompose it. This process releases nutrients back into the soil, and these nutrients are used by growing plants. The decomposers themselves are food for forest animals such as birds, lizards and spiders.

Billions of beetles

There are more species of beetle than there are species of any other type of animal. Many beetle species are found in leaf litter. A study of a mixed temperate forest in California, in the United States, found 287 species of beetles living in the leaf litter.

Temperate forest ecosystems

Living and non-living things, and the **interactions** between them, make up temperate forest **ecosystems**. Living things are plants, fungi and animals. Non-living things are the soil, the leaf litter and the **climate**.

Food chains and food webs

A very important way that different **species** interact is by eating or consuming other species. This transfers energy and **nutrients** from one **organism** to another. A food chain illustrates this flow of energy, by showing what eats what. Food chains are best set out in a diagram. A food web shows how many different food chains fit together.

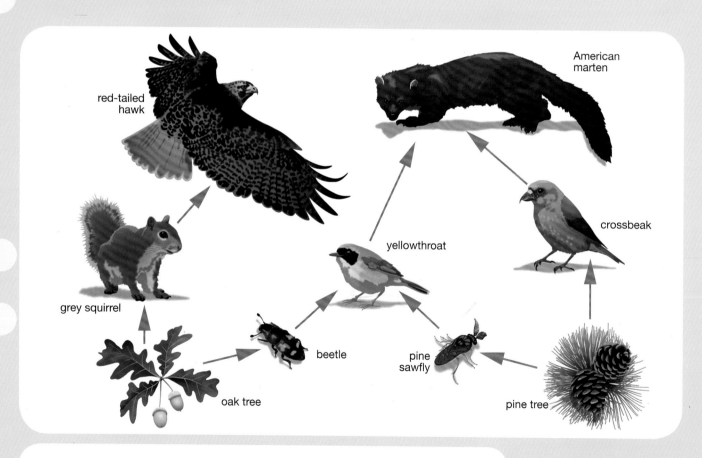

This North American mixed forest food web is made up of several food chains. In one food chain, oak trees are eaten by grey squirrels, which in turn are eaten by red-tailed hawks.

Other interactions

Non-living and living things in a temperate forest interact in other ways, too. In the forests of North America, fires burn in summer, killing tree seedlings and many animals. After the trees have burned, more light reaches the ground, and grasses grow densely in the ash of the leaf litter. Grazing animals such as deer come to feed on the grass, and as the grass matures, seed-eaters such as mice arrive. In turn, **predators** such as owls and coyotes are attracted to the forest to hunt and feed.

Temperature and day length affect **migratory** birds and **hibernating** bears. When the days get shorter and the air gets cooler in autumn, many birds fly south to warmer places. Black bears dig their dens and begin their long hibernation. In spring, the bears emerge, ready to feed. The birds return in spring, too.

Fires are a natural part of many temperate forest ecosystems in the United States and Australia.

Did you know?

Summer fires in the temperate forests of California and south-eastern Australia are the fiercest of any fires in the world. Dry air, fuel and high temperatures create ideal conditions for fires, which are started by humans or by lightning strikes.

Threats to temperate forests

Temperate forests around the world are under threat from activities such as land-clearing and **invasive species**. Many native species lose their **habitats** and face **extinction**.

Biodiversity hotspots

There are about 34 regions in the world that have been identified as biodiversity hotspots. These hotspots are regions that have very high biodiversity that is under severe threat from human activities. Biodiversity hotspots have many **endemic species**. The whole of New Zealand is considered a biodiversity hotspot, including its temperate forests.

New Zealand kauri forests

New Zealand's temperate kauri forests are located in the far north of its North Island. Kauri trees can live for 2000 years and grow 40 metres tall. Their trunks can be more than 4 metres thick.

Many endemic tree species grow in a kauri forest, along with endemic ferns and grasses. The North Island kiwi and kokako are endemic bird species, and the kauri snail is a large, meat-eating endemic species. New Zealand's only two native mammals are found in the kauri forests. Both are bat species.

Tāne Mahuta is the largest kauri tree in the biodiversity hotspot of New Zealand. It is 51 metres tall and between 1250 and 2500 years old.

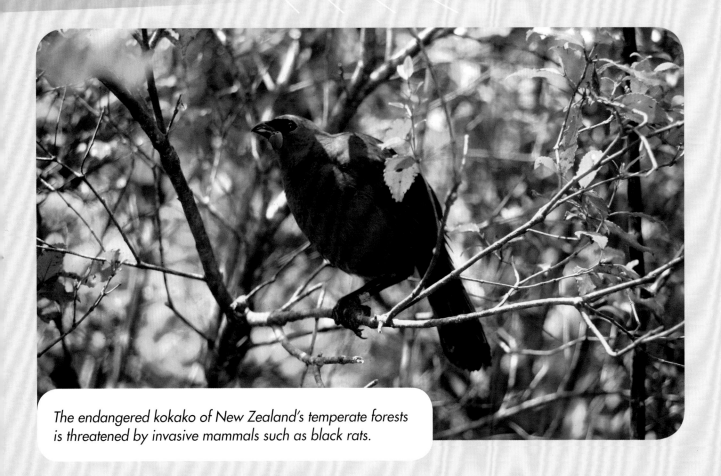

The endangered kokako of New Zealand's temperate forests is threatened by invasive mammals such as black rats.

Threats to kauri forest biodiversity

Kauri forests once covered 12 000 square kilometres of New Zealand. Land-clearing for farming has reduced this area to just 800 square kilometres.

Today, invasive species are the greatest threat to kauri forest biodiversity. In the 1800s, European settlers introduced 34 mammal species into New Zealand. Many of these mammals, including stoats, weasels, black rats, dogs and cats, are **predators** that prey on native birds and their eggs. Other invasive species, such as deer and brushtail possums, heavily graze many kauri forest plants.

Conserving kauri forest biodiversity

Today, kauri forests are protected from land-clearing. In some areas, cleared land has been replanted with kauri species.

To conserve the forests' biodiversity, invasive species control must continue. New Zealand has a lot of expertise in invasive animal control. Pests such as rats, rabbits and stoats have been removed from many islands so that endangered native animals can thrive on the islands. Some threatened native species have been relocated to these pest-free islands so that they are safe from invasive species, too.

BIODIVERSITY THREAT:
Agriculture

Temperate forests grow in places that have good soil, plentiful water and a mild **climate**. These places are also best suited to agriculture, so it is not surprising that large areas of temperate forest across the world have been cleared for farming.

Effects on biodiversity

Habitats are destroyed when temperate forests are cleared for agriculture. Some **species** can become **extinct**. Red squirrels in Britain cannot survive without forest, because they can only find food and shelter in forest trees.

Clearing forest for farming creates new habitats. Some forest animals can take advantage of these changes. A badger can gather food in open farmland, but it needs enough forest to be able to dig burrows, called setts, for shelter and breeding. Deer, too, will graze in open farmland but use patches of forest for shelter.

Clearing for farmland creates open habitats, which are the preferred habitats of merlins and magpies. These birds increase in number, but wood warblers and treecreepers lose their habitats and their population falls.

Europeans began to clear forests in north-eastern United States after the arrival of English settlers aboard the Mayflower in 1620. Three hundred years later, most of the temperate forest had been cleared for farmland.

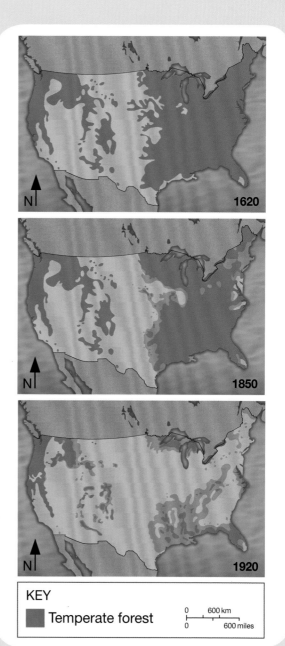

1620

1850

1920

KEY

Temperate forest

0   600 km
0   600 miles

Fragmented habitats

Trees that are on even ground are often cleared for agriculture, leaving fragments or patches of forest on steep slopes where farming machinery cannot reach. Forest patches are important habitats for many species, but many animals cannot move between patches to breed outside their groups. In time, animals in a group may become inbred and closely related to one another. This loss of **genetic** diversity makes the species vulnerable to disease, because individuals are very similar and if one is affected by disease, it is likely that all will become affected.

When land is cleared for farming, this creates fragmented forest habitats. Each fragment of forest is isolated and many animals are stranded, as if on islands.

To help stop inbreeding, strips of forest can be replanted along creeks and ridges, linking the islands of forest habitat. These strips are called wildlife corridors. They allow animals from different patches to meet and interbreed.

Loss of knowledge

All over the world, indigenous people have used forest plants for a variety of purposes, from food to medicine to insect repellent. This knowledge has been gathered over many hundreds of years. In the past, a lot of this knowledge was lost when new settlers removed indigenous people from their lands and cleared forests for farming.

BIODIVERSITY THREAT:
Invasive species

Introduced **species** are non-native species that are introduced accidentally or deliberately into a **habitat**. If they thrive and spread, they become **invasive species**. Invasive species threaten the biodiversity of temperate forests.

How are species introduced?

Some invasive species are introduced into forests deliberately. The brushtail possum was taken to New Zealand from Australia in 1837 to be grown for its fur. By 1860, it was widespread in New Zealand's forests.

Some species are brought deliberately into a new country, but then escape into other habitats. Runaway pet cats may become **feral** and hunt forest animals. European honeybees can escape from their hives to form wild hives in forests. These insects compete with native bees and birds for nectar. An introduced plant can spread from gardens when its seed is carried by the wind or spread in bird droppings. There may be no diseases that kill the plant species and no animals that eat it. This means it could spread uncontrollably.

The brushtail possum is protected in Australia, but it is a serious pest in New Zealand, where it was introduced.

The destruction of the American chestnut

In the past in some forests of the eastern United States, one in four trees was an American chestnut tree. This tree grows to a height of 50 metres, and its wood was widely used for building. Sometime soon after 1900, the species began to die out. The trees were being killed by chestnut blight fungus, an **organism** native to Japan and China. The fungus was probably introduced to New York State through infected wood or imported trees. It spread quickly.

By 1940, almost all of an estimated 4 billion American chestnut trees had been killed. Today, blight-resistant trees are being bred from the few specimens that survived. The American Chestnut Foundation is a conservation organisation that replants these trees in areas that were once chestnut forest.

Did you know?

The European gypsy moth, the sirex wood wasp from Asia and Europe, and the Asian longhorned beetle are just some of the introduced insect species that attack forest trees in the eastern United States.

Some invasive species of temperate forests

SPECIES	ORIGIN	WHERE IT WAS INTRODUCED	HOW IT WAS INTRODUCED	BIODIVERSITY THREAT
English ivy	Europe	South-eastern Australia and parts of the United States	As a garden plant	Smothers ground plants
Japanese climbing fern	Japan	South-eastern United States	As a garden plant	Smothers forest plants
Domestic cat	Europe	Many countries	As a pet	Preys on native species
Brushtail possum	Australia	New Zealand	To begin a fur trade	Eats many forest plants

BIODIVERSITY THREAT:
Logging

Temperate forests have been harvested for their timber for hundreds of years. Today, in many countries, logging continues to be a major threat to the biodiversity of these forests.

Types of logging

There are different ways of logging a forest. Some forests, or parts of forests, are clear-felled, which means that every tree in the area is cut down. Once the logs are removed, the remaining wood and small plants may be burned to encourage regrowth. Other forests are selectively logged. This means that only the trees that are commercially valuable are cut down.

Short-term effects of logging

Whichever way a forest is logged, its biodiversity is affected in many ways. The use of heavy machinery damages the **understorey** and forest soil. It kills animals and destroys their burrows and nests. Roads are built, allowing introduced plants and animals to be carried into the forest by logging trucks. More dirt enters forest streams and they become filled with **silt**.

Logging changes forest **habitats** completely and has both short-term and long-term effects on biodiversity.

Conservationists try to help Leadbeater's possums by installing nest boxes in forests where trees are too young to have natural hollows.

Long-term effects of logging

Logging changes the plant composition of a forest. Natural forests usually contain both young and old trees, but when an area is clear-felled, the trees that regrow are of the same age. This is unsuitable habitat for some animal **species** and this can have long-term effects. Leadbeater's possum is a small, endangered marsupial of south-eastern Australia that needs forest habitats that have many young trees, a few old trees and a dense understorey of acacia trees. The possum feeds on insects and sap from young trees, and it shelters and breeds in nest hollows in old trees. The acacias provide it with safe crossing points between trees. These possums are losing their habitats because replanted forests do not have a mix of trees.

Carolina parakeet

On 21 February 1918, the last known specimen of the Carolina parakeet died at Cincinnati Zoo in Ohio, in the United States. This species was the only parrot species native to the eastern United States. The logging of its forest habitat was the main cause of its **extinction**.

BIODIVERSITY THREAT:
Climate change

The world's average temperature is rising because levels of certain gases, such as **carbon dioxide**, are increasing in Earth's atmosphere. The temperature increase is causing other **climate** changes. These changes affect temperate forest **habitats**.

Effects of climate change on forests

Scientists are uncertain exactly how temperate forests will be affected by climate change. They do know that the amount of rainfall and where it falls will change. Scientists predict that in general the United States will become warmer and wetter over the next 50 years. This should increase the area of temperate forest. In the south-east and south-west of the United States, however, rainfall is predicted to decrease. This would lead to an increase in the number and intensity of fires, causing forests to be replaced by woodlands, shrublands and grasslands.

Invasive species

Climate change will affect the distribution of introduced plants and animals in forests. In Australia, an increase in temperature will probably allow the introduced plant lantana to spread southward into wet forests. With reduced rainfall, an introduced plant pest called gorse is likely to retreat south. This is because gorse cannot tolerate very dry conditions.

Temperate forests in the United States should increase in size as the climate becomes warmer and wetter.

Bark beetles bore into trees and lay their eggs, then their young feed on the bark and wood, which can kill the trees. Climate change is causing beetle populations to grow.

Bark beetles

Since 1990, bark beetles have killed millions of trees in temperate forests along the western coast of North America. Bark beetle **species** are native to these forests, but their effects have never been so severe. Scientists believe that a rise in average temperatures has meant that beetles survive longer and reproduce more, and reduced rainfall has weakened the trees' resistance to beetle attack.

Disease

Red band needle blight is a fungal disease that has recently become a serious threat to lodgepole pines in British Columbia, in Canada. The spread of this disease is due to an increase in summer rainfall, which allows the fungus to thrive.

Did you know?

Earth's climate has changed many times over millions of years. About 10 000 years ago, during the last ice age, most of Canada and northern Europe were covered in icesheets that were 3 kilometres thick.

Temperate forest conservation

Conservation is the protection, preservation and wise use of resources. Temperate forests are a valuable resource and their biodiversity needs to be conserved. Research, education, laws and breeding programs all play a part in forest conservation.

Research

Research projects are carried out to find out information about temperate forest **ecosystems**. This information shows us why forest ecosystems are important, and it helps people make decisions about how to protect forests and their biodiversity. Scientific studies have shown that temperate forests store more carbon per hectare than rainforests do. When these forests are cleared and burned, the carbon is released into the atmosphere as **carbon dioxide**, adding to **climate** change. Conserving temperate forests means that carbon remains stored and is not released.

The importance of temperate forests

Temperate forests are very important for many reasons. They:

- are **habitat** for many animal **species**
- are wondrous places to visit
- absorb carbon dioxide and release oxygen
- filter pollutants from water and bind the soil, preventing **erosion**.

Amount of carbon stored by different types of forest

TYPE OF FOREST	AVERAGE AMOUNT OF CARBON STORED PER HECTARE (TONNES)
Temperate *Eucalyptus regnans* forests of south-eastern Australia	2 844
Temperate forests in high rainfall areas	377
Subtropical forests	294
Temperate forests in low rainfall areas	176
Tropical rainforests	171

Education

Educating people about temperate forests is essential for forest conservation. Information from scientists must be passed on to people, such as students, loggers and tourists. When people are shown how temperate forests are important to their own lives, they are more likely to help conserve them.

Protected areas and breeding programs

Temperate forest habitat may be protected by national parks and reserves, and this helps to conserve forest wildlife too. Breeding programs in zoos can save temperate forest species from **extinction**. These programs are necessary when a species' numbers are very low or when its habitat is endangered. Animals bred in zoos may be released back into the wild if areas of suitable habitat exist.

The highly endangered Iberian lynx lives in Mediterranean forest in Spain. These animals are being bred in captivity, and scientists plan to reintroduce them into the wild to increase the small population.

Laws to protect forest species

In Tasmania, in Australia, the government passed a law that all pet cats must be desexed, so that they cannot breed, and microchipped, so that they can be identified electronically. This is to stop **feral** cat numbers growing. There are more than 150 000 feral cats in Tasmania, and these cats prey on native forest species.

CASE STUDY:
The Bialowieza Forest

The Bialowieza Forest covers 1500 square kilometres of Poland and Belarus. Unlike other European forests, it has been mostly undisturbed by humans. Because of this, it has many **species** that are found nowhere else in Europe.

Bialowieza Forest biodiversity

Bialowieza Forest is the last wild **habitat** of Europe's largest mammal, the wisent, also called the European bison. Other rare mammals of the forest are the European lynx, European badger, grey wolf, elk, otter and masked shrew.

The main evergreen tree species in the Bialowieza Forest are conifers, such as Scots pine and Norway spruce. The main deciduous species are aspen, white birch, hornbeam, English oak, alder, linden, lime, goat willow, Norway maple and ash.

Numbers of known species in Bialowieza Forest

TYPE OF **ORGANISM**	KNOWN SPECIES
Animals	At least 12 000
Insects	More than 8 500
Birds	232
Mammals	62
Amphibians	12
Reptiles	7
Plants	At least 1 400
Liverworts (type of small, flowerless plant)	800
Vascular plants (a plant that has veins that carry water and **nutrients** through its stems and leaves)	632
Fungi	More than 3 000
Lichen	254

Ancient home of wisents

The Bialowieza Forest is the last remaining part of the deciduous and mixed temperate forest that once covered much of Europe. It is around 10 000 years old. Other forests in Europe have been cleared but Bialowieza Forest has been protected, in different ways, for the past 600 years. This protection began in the 1400s when King Władysław Jagiełło banned hunting and tree-cutting in the forest, so that he would have wisents to hunt. The kings and tsars who followed him also protected the wisent and its habitat.

During World War I (1914–18), German troops occupied the forest. They shot forest animals such as wisents for food. By 1919, the wisent was **extinct** in the wild.

In the 1920s, a breeding program was begun to save the species, using 54 wisents from zoos and private collections. In 1929, 53 square kilometres of the forest was made a national park and a few wisents were released. Today, more than 540 wisents live in the forest.

Wisent numbers in the Bialowieza Forest are recovering as a result of a breeding program.

27

World Heritage Site

The **heritage** importance of Bialowieza Forest biodiversity is recognised by the United Nations. In 1971, an area of 48 square kilometres at the centre of the Bialowieza Forest National Park was named as a **World Heritage Site**. In 1992, another 45 square kilometres was added. In 1996, the total area of national parks in Poland was increased to 105 square kilometres.

Protecting the forest

Despite its World Heritage listing, only about 10 per cent of the Bialowieza Forest is fully protected from logging and hunting. The national parks in Poland and Belarus cover just 152 square kilometres of forest. Within the park boundaries, there are areas where no vehicles are permitted. These areas have been set aside for special protection, because vehicles compact the soil, disturb wildlife and carry in weed seeds on their tyres. Today, logging and hunting continue in the forest outside the national parks.

Some parts of the Bialowieza Forest that are not protected have been cleared by farmers for crops. Conservation organisations such as the World Wide Fund for Nature (WWF) are campaigning to achieve full protection for the entire forest.

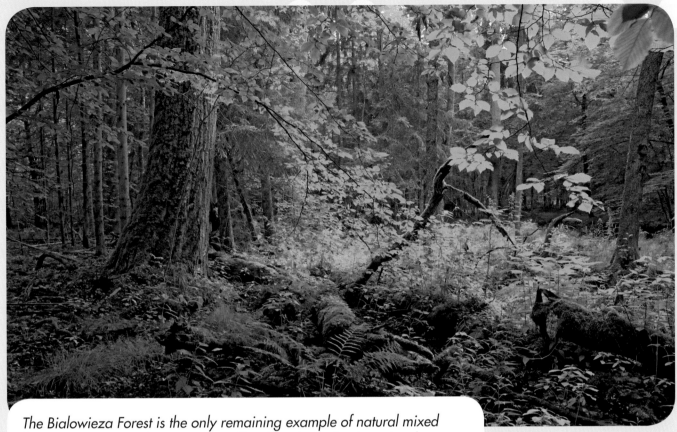

The Bialowieza Forest is the only remaining example of natural mixed forest in Europe, so the protection offered by the Bialowieza Development Program is very important.

Bialowieza Development Program

In 2009, a conference about the conservation of Bialowieza Forest took place in the national park. Scientists, local people, the United Nations, conservation organisations and the Polish and Belarusian governments attended the conference. The Bialowieza Development Program (BDP) was announced and official agreements were signed. The BDP aims to triple the area of protected forest, and also develop industries that provide work for local people but which do not damage the forest or its biodiversity.

The importance of the Bialowieza Forest

Professor Alan Weisman, a science writer, spoke about Bialowieza Forest at the BDP conference. He said that it is:

'one of the oldest intact forests anywhere … it provides a baseline of what healthy temperate forests might have been like. A baseline is an invaluable tool, because from one we can track changes, especially changes caused by human activity, far more easily than we can in a forest that has been severely altered by humans …'

What is the future for temperate forests?

Temperate forests are under severe threat from human activities. It may seem impossible to stop their destruction, but when threats are removed, biodiversity decline can be slowed or stopped. Some **species** may reappear and increase biodiversity.

What can you do for temperate forests?

You can help protect forests in several ways.

- Find out about temperate forests. Why are they important and what threatens them?
- If you live in or near a forest, you can join volunteer groups who replant cleared land with forest species.
- Become a responsible consumer. Do not litter and do not buy products that have been harvested from forests.
- If you are concerned about forests in your area, or beyond, write to or email your local newspaper, your local member of parliament or another politician. Know what you want to say, set out your arguments, be sure of your facts and ask for a reply.

Useful websites

🖥 **http://wwf.panda.org/about_our_earth/ecoregions/about/habitat_types/habitats/temperate_forests**
This WWF website contains information about temperate forest **habitats**, **ecosystems** and wildlife.

🖥 **http://www.biodiversityhotspots.org**
This website has information about the richest and most threatened areas of biodiversity on Earth.

🖥 **http://www.iucnredlist.org**
The IUCN Red List has information about threatened plant and animal species.

Glossary

adapt   change in order to survive

canopy   leaves of the upper layer of plants in a forest or woodland

carbon dioxide   a colourless and odourless gas produced by plants and animals

climate   the weather conditions in a certain region over a long period of time

domestic   tame and kept or cultivated by humans

ecosystem   the living and non-living things in a certain area and the interactions between them

endemic species   species found only in a particular area

erosion   wearing away of soil and rock by wind or water

extinct   having no living members

feral   wild, especially domestic animals that have gone wild

fertile   capable of producing lots of vegetation, possibly due to a high nutrient content

gene   segment of deoxyribonucleic acid (DNA) in the cells of a living thing, which determines its characteristics

habitat   place where animals, plants or other living things live

heritage   things we inherit and pass on to following generations

hibernate   spend the winter in a dormant state (as if in a deep sleep) to conserve energy

interaction   action that is taken together or actions that affect each other

invasive species   non-native species that spread through habitats

migrate   move from one place to another, especially seasonally

nutrient   chemical that is used by living things for growth

organism   animal, plant or other living thing

predator   animal that kills and eats other animals

silt   soil and sediments carried in water

species   a group of animals, plants or other living things that share the same characteristics and can breed with one another

tropical   in the hot and humid region between the Tropic of Cancer and the Tropic of Capricorn

understorey   layer of plants that grows below the canopy of a forest

vegetation   plants

World Heritage Site   a site that is recognised as having great international importance and that is protected by the United Nations Educational, Scientific and Cultural Organization (UNESCO)

Index